T0130242

THE INTERWOVEN LIFE

"God has a plan for your life and will put it together piece by piece until it is complete".

GARY L. VERNON

Copyright © 2021 Gary L. Vernon.

All rights reserved. No part of this book may be used or reproduced by any means, graphic, electronic, or mechanical, including photocopying, recording, taping or by any information storage retrieval system without the written permission of the author except in the case of brief quotations embodied in critical articles and reviews.

WestBow Press books may be ordered through booksellers or by contacting:

WestBow Press
A Division of Thomas Nelson & Zondervan
1663 Liberty Drive
Bloomington, IN 47403
www.westbowpress.com
844-714-3454

Because of the dynamic nature of the Internet, any web addresses or links contained in this book may have changed since publication and may no longer be valid. The views expressed in this work are solely those of the author and do not necessarily reflect the views of the publisher, and the publisher hereby disclaims any responsibility for them.

Any people depicted in stock imagery provided by Getty Images are models, and such images are being used for illustrative purposes only. Certain stock imagery © Getty Images.

Scripture quotations taken from The Holy Bible, New International Version® NIV® Copyright © 1973 1978 1984 2011 by Biblica, Inc. TM. Used by permission. All rights reserved worldwide.

Scripture taken from the New King James Version® Copyright © 1982 by Thomas Nelson. Used by permission. All rights reserved.

Scripture taken from the King James Version of the Bible.

ISBN: 978-1-6642-2194-9 (sc)
ISBN: 978-1-6642-2195-6 (e)

Library of Congress Control Number: 2021901928

Print information available on the last page.

WestBow Press rev. date: 04/09/2021

CONTENTS

THE INTERWOVEN LIFE

God has a plan for your life.
What happens when you surrender yourself fully to Him?
This is the story of a seven- year- old boy who was called to preach and whose life
was amazingly interwoven by God through over 60 years of ministry.

"For I know the plans I have for you," declares the LORD, "plans to prosper you and
not to harm you, plans to give you hope and a future." Jeremiah 29:11 (NIV)

INTRODUCTION

God has a plan for your life, interweaving strand by strand, until it has been interwoven to completion. God first spoke to me at age seven and I preached my first sermon shortly thereafter. By age 12, I was traveling by bus during the summer months conducting revivals throughout churches in Virginia.

At 15 years of age, I was asked to briefly fill my first pulpit in Buena Vista, Virginia. By age 16, due to the death of the former pastor, I was sent to pastor a small country church in Winfall, Virginia. Following that assignment, I would pastor Brookneal, Danville, Poplar Camp and Lynchburg, all in Virginia.

Over this span of time we have watched God do some amazing things. This book contains many of our life experiences in short story format.

It is my hope that you will enjoy reading these reflections and that you will find this book an inspiration to you on your journey through life. God has a plan for you and He has already begun *to weave the strands of your life together.*

GOD, I'M ONLY SEVEN

There was nothing unusual about this day. I had played all day like any seven-year-old would do. It came bed time and my two brothers and I had moved into a room downstairs due to the extremely cold weather. Normally, I would go right to sleep but this night I was restless and feeling like something unusual was happening. My brothers had gone to sleep. Suddenly I clearly heard my name called. Actually, it was a little frightening. I thought one of my brothers had called me. I decided to try going to sleep again. As I closed my eyes I heard that same voice calling out my name. It frightened me so badly that I got up and went to my parents' room and asked if they had called me. My parents did not realize what was happening in the life of their youngest son and told me to go back to bed and try going to sleep. As I closed my eyes a third time I heard the voice call my name again but this time the voice said, "I am calling you to preach." I knew Who this was by then and I remember saying to God, "I can't do this. I'm just a seven-year-old kid!" This calling was one of the most dramatic things that ever happened in my life. It set my future life in motion and I knew God had a plan for me.

Many times, when I was tired, distressed or frustrated I always ended up going back to that night and it always brought re-assurance. Your calling may not happen the way God called me, but we need to know that our calling is sure.

A Passion for Souls :

It was not long after I was called to preach that I got my dad's old reel to reel tape recorder and went to the church to practice preaching a sermon. It went alright for a seven-year-old. I couldn't wait to take the recorder to the house and play my sermonette to dad. I believe for the first time he realized that God had his hand on me and was ***weaving my life together***. He asked if I would like to preach at church and I agreed. I chose a sermon out of my Bible story book entitled, "The Tower of Pride." (Tower of Babel) The entire sermon lasted about five minutes. Some who heard that sermon told me in later years how much they would love to hear one of those *"five- minute sermons"* again. At the end of that sermon a young girl about my age came to the altar and gave her heart to the Lord. I still hear from her occasionally after over 60 years. That first convert sowed a passion for souls in my heart that is still alive today.

BUENA VISTA-1967

I was asked to fill the pulpit until after the state convention. There were some beautiful people there including the Farley family. Their daughter, Saundra is now a member at the Lynchburg church. I had the honor of preaching Brother and Sister Farley's funeral

WINFALL
FEBRUARY '68-AUGUST '69

I was appointed as pastor following the death of the previous pastor. These were absolutely great people and we formed lasting relationships. They were so good to me and I shall never forget their kindness. Barbara, one of the children there, is now at Lynchburg and serves as our Senior Saints director. Ava, the pianist there is now pastoring a church.

Pastor at Winfall church with 12 members and carrying a Million Miler briefcase with nothing in it but a one-sheet sermon.

BROOKNEAL
JANUARY '71-JULY '72

We have so many wonderful memories from Brookneal. God blessed us with growth and the little sanctuary was often full. Alma and I were married while pastoring there. I have returned to preach many funerals and we keep in touch.

DANVILLE 1974-1979

Danville was our first full time church. We have many fine memories of the wonderful people who were there. Our first child was born during this pastorate. My father, H.E. Vernon was the former pastor and he died during our pastorate. God blessed us with several accomplishments during our time there.

POPLAR CAMP 1979-1989

Returning, as pastor, to the place where I grew up as a child was exciting. The Poplar Camp people were genuine and committed. God blessed us tremendously during our ten-year pastorate there. Our daughter was born while we were there. Poplar Camp will always be special to us.

LYNCHBURG 1989- PRESENT

How blessed we have been to pastor at Lynchburg for the past 31 years. My teen years were spent here and it is where I met my wife. We hold so many memories from this church. We thank God for the many friends and relationships we have made. You will always hold a special place in our hearts.

INSPIRATIONAL GEMS

When Small Is Great:

Christmas was our favorite time of the year at the Poplar Camp Church. On the night of our Christmas program all the gifts were handed out from under the tree. I sat on the front pew and waited with anticipation for them to call my name. Gift after gift was called and I was starting to feel very disappointed. I watched as the gifts got down to three, two and then down to the last gift. They picked it up and called out "Gary Vernon." It was from Granny Martin. When I opened it, inside was a red rubber ball. I was thrilled to just receive a present. I played with that ball until it literally came apart. Of all the great gifts I have received that is the one I remember most. Even in this day of plenty, don't underestimate the value of a small gift.

I Believe in Angels:

My dad had left for the day and I woke up with a very high fever. I was seeing all sorts of images but there was one I remember to this day. It was a picture puzzle of the United States. I would fill in all the states until the last one. When I put in the last piece, the map would blow up and I would have to start all over again. I was actually delirious with fever. My mom called Brother Carpenter, a minister in our church, to come and pray for me. I barely remember him being there but heard him when he started praying. When he laid his hand on my head, I felt the healing virtue. Just as that happened, I looked up and there was a very bright light in the corner of the room, next to the ceiling. I was immediately healed and before Brother Carpenter left I was playing with my toys. There is not a doubt in my mind that the bright light was an angel and that angel was on a healing mission that morning. I was healed!

My first bible

A Special Convert:

When I was a young man I was asked to be the evangelist at a youth camp in Leesville. We had some great services each night. One night the Spirit came down in our midst and filled the house. Many of the campers were saved including a young girl from Lynchburg by the name of Alma Smith. I jokingly said later, "If I had known then that she would one day become my wife, I would have prayed with her longer."

Whosoever Will:

Brother Vernil Sides, one of my mentors and good friends, was pastoring in Alabama and invited me to come for a revival. I prayed about it and decided I would go. We had a wonderful revival and it was a joy to stay with the Sides in their home. During that revival a young man, who was of the Catholic faith, came to the altar and was saved by grace. As often happens, once the revival ended, I moved on to the next revival.

I often wondered what happened to him. Years later Brother Sides was at the General Assembly and ran into that young Catholic man. He was married and had a family and was still excited about serving the Lord! Praise God! It is stories like this that makes you want to excel in soul-winning.

Almost Persuaded:

I was conducting a week's revival at the Java church. One night as I was preaching I became very burdened for a young man sitting in the back of the church. I finished the sermon and several people came forward to seek God. He was still sitting in the back and did not seem interested in wanting to come. At that point I could hardly bear the burden upon me and decided to go back and talk with him. He was mannerly and seemed like a nice young man. The burden persisted and I talked with him a little more. He said he would not come that night. I went back to the pulpit and he finally went out. The burden got even heavier and I know the voice of the Lord directed me to go outside and try one more time. That may have been the only time I ever went outside to pray with someone as the church continued to pray inside. I felt his blood was on my hands. I went out not knowing whether he was still there or had left. He was sitting in his car. I walked up to his car and told him about the heavy burden I was feeling for him. He seemed appreciative for my concern but he just would not submit. I went back inside and shortly thereafter the service concluded. The revival ended and I returned to Lynchburg. It wasn't long before I received a phone call that this young man had died in a terrible car accident. As far as we know he never did accept the Lord into his life. I was very grieved to hear the news but it was then that I realized why God was so persistent that I witness to him that night. This could have been a great story with a great ending but not everybody is going to accept Christ. I was glad I went the extra mile that night.

"Then Agrippa said unto Paul, almost thou persuadest me to be a Christian." Acts 26:28 KJV

The Blessing of Failure:

When I was in middle school I took a class in Biology. I liked Biology and found it interesting but I was at that age when I just didn't study and apply myself. I was not very fond of my teacher and just cruised along. By year's end I realized I was likely going to fail the class. Sure enough I failed my only class ever. My end score missed passing by one point. I talked to the teacher and asked if he would give me that point but he wouldn't budge. Suddenly I had a flashback to something that happened months back. He made the statement that humans came from monkeys and I spoke up and said, "Maybe you came from a monkey but I didn't!" There went *that point* I so needed to pass, but I got to speak my peace. Failing that class was a wakeup call for me and I determined I would never let that happen again. From that time forward I never failed a class. In fact, soon I was on the honor roll. Thank you, teacher, for turning my life around. *I got the point* after all.

Good Deeds Can Pay Big Dividends:

When I was in high school I had to take a class in Algebra. I never did understand Algebra and never could figure out where it would fit into the work I would be doing as a minister. I lost interest and more or less just sat through the class. School was about to end for the year and I had a failing grade. My teacher was very old and was retiring. It was the last day of school and I was walking down the hallway and glanced into her classroom. She was cleaning out her desk and had boxes and bags ready to load. I really felt sorry for her and just walked in and asked if she needed any help. She was so grateful, and likely stunned, but she said she would really appreciate it. I loaded all the items for her and the last thing she had in her hand was her grade book. She said, "Vernon" (she always called me by my last name) "I was looking through the gradebook and I made a mistake on your final grade." She marked out the "F" and put a "D". I thanked her and never saw her again. I never offered my help with that in mind but it sure was a blessing.

Miracle on Otey Street:

After I returned home from college, our band moved into an apartment in Lynchburg. We scheduled some weekend revivals in the state of Virginia. This particular day we were supposed to leave for Newport News for a revival but we had one big problem. We had no money to buy gas for the trip. It was getting later and later and we did not know what to do. I told everyone we needed to pray. Not long afterward, there was a knock on the door. That was very unusual since not many people knew where we lived. When I opened the door, it was Emmit Mitchel, a man who attended the Winfall church years back. I asked him what he was doing there and he said he just felt like we needed some money. This was an absolute answer to prayer. He gave us enough money to fill up my gas tank and we had enough for all of us to eat at McDonald's. God answers prayer!

Singing on TV:

While in the coastal area of Virginia the band we brought from college had an opportunity to be on the PTL television program with Pat Robertson. We recorded four to five songs. That was an experience for sure. When we left we went to a restaurant to eat. Upon arrival we noticed they had a round platform in the center of the stage. We introduced ourselves and asked if we could sing a few songs. I'll never forget the song we sang, "Don't overlook salvation while searching for great joy, He's knocking at your heart's door, let Him in." One of the waitresses was waiting on tables when she suddenly broke out in tears and began weeping. God was dealing with her. She went in the kitchen and did not come back out so we did not get to talk with her. That was an amazing night! I often pray for God to give me greater passion and boldness.

A Timely Gift:

The night Alma and I got married we had very little money so we planned to spend one night away before going back to Brookneal. Some honeymoon, huh? Just before the wedding began one of my dearest friends, Buena Mitchell, came back to the room where we were waiting and handed me a nice money gift. We ended up having a three-day honeymoon and got to visit Lurray Caverns. To this day I miss Buena. She was my confidant when I pastored Winfall. Isn't it amazing how God works things out? *He was weaving more strands into my life.*

Hearing the Voice of God:

I was just walking through the house when God urged me to visit a member of my church. I had no idea why I needed to go but God just kept prompting me, so I told my wife that we had to go visit this home. We got into the car and drove to their house. I rang the doorbell and the member came to the door and looked stunned that we were there. We were invited in and I told them about how God prompted us to come. The person began to weep and told us they had been praying about a decision and they had asked God to send us. It was awesome how God worked that out. Many times, I have wondered what would have happened if I had not listened to God.

Sin Exposed:

We were in a revival at the Danville church and were praying for various people in the altar when God prompted my heart that something was going on in the basement. The prompting was so strong that I went to see what it was all about. As I entered the basement, I didn't see anything unusual but opened each door of the Sunday School rooms. They were all dark. I started second-guessing myself and just wrote it off. I went back upstairs where the praying was still going on and once again the Spirit prompted me that I needed to go back to the basement and check things out. The prompting was so strong that I immediately went back. Once again, I saw nothing unusual but proceeded to check each room but this time I turned the light on in the rooms. When I got to the last room I turned the light on and there was a young couple engaging in inappropriate behavior. We had a stern brief talk and I told them to get upstairs immediately. You can't hide from God. Be sure your sins will find you out.

Unscheduled Prayer Service:

Years ago, while pastoring at Poplar Camp, my phone rang one day and on the other end of the line was a desperate mother asking if I could come and pray with her two teenage sons. Immediately my wife and I were on the way. When I entered the door, I saw the two young men and they were looking very somber. Both of them were under conviction. I asked if they wanted to be saved and we prayed together for some time. God was in the house! I became good friends with both of them and it was always good to see them in church. Over thirty years had passed and I was on my way to Troutville to serve on the State Review Board. To my pleasant surprise, one of the candidates was Tony and he was scheduled to appear before the board to apply for a deacon's license.

Seeing him reminded me of the day I came to their house and prayed with them. He said, "That was the day I accepted Christ as my Savior." That absolutely made my day.

Meanest Man in Town:

While pastoring at Poplar Camp I heard about a man who was very sick in the hospital. I mentioned that I was going to visit him and someone said, "you are wasting your time with that man. You will be doing good if he even lets you come into the room." Something kept urging me to go see this man so I drove to Pulaski Hospital and located his room. I got the impression that he really didn't want a visitor, much less a minister. I held my ground and talked very candidly to him about his need for accepting the Lord. He said he wouldn't do it right then but I could tell he was pondering this decision. I left that day feeling a little dejected because I felt God had prompted me to go. The next day I still had this man on my mind so I drove back to Pulaski to visit him again. I walked into the room and before I could say "Hello" he said, "Guess what happened last night?" I asked him "what?" He boldly and happily said, "I prayed that prayer and accepted Christ as my Savior!" Needless to say, I was overjoyed! The giant wicked man in Wythe County had given his life to Christ! The bigger they are the harder they fall.

My Visit to Heaven:

A bishop from general headquarters was at the Poplar Camp church to teach a course and preach. That Sunday evening, I felt a need to go to the church and pray. I ended up praying in the nursery. After a while, I went from my knees to laying down on the floor. That day I had one of the most amazing visions I've ever experienced. As I was praying it was like something lifted me up and the next thing I knew I was at the pearly gates. Suddenly the doors opened and I was able to glance inside. It was the brightest, most beautiful place I've ever experienced. There was a peace there that I cannot describe. I wanted to go in but suddenly I came back to reality. When I realized that I was still on this earth I began to weep uncontrollably that I was back in this world. I had tasted of heaven and wanted to stay. Heaven will surely be worth it all.

Stretching Your Money:

While I was at Poplar Camp a senior lady asked to talk with me. She was a good lady and loved the Lord. She was a widow and it seemed she was struggling financially and could barely make ends meet. I honestly felt bad for her. Then she told me that she did not have enough money left over after paying her bills to pay tithes. She asked me if I thought that was ok. Rather than giving her a point-blank response I shared some stories with her of how God had blessed other people who were faithful tithers. While I understood her circumstances, I still felt obligated to encourage her to tithe. I told her that I would not tell anyone not to tithe. She left the meeting and nothing else was mentioned. Later one Sunday, she called me aside and said she had something to tell me. Her eyes were lit up and she had a peaceful look on her face. She said, "Pastor, I started paying tithes right after our talk a few months ago," and she said, "Honestly, I've had no financial problems since." She said that once she started tithing, she had more money than before. I've used this story many times when talking to others about the need for tithing.

Saying Goodbye to a Pet:

People's love for their pets is real. We now have pet cemeteries, doctors specializing in pets and even funerals for pets. One day our phone rang at Poplar Camp and it was Doug and Peggy, calling to tell me their beloved beautiful cat, Fluffy, had died. It sounded like they were weeping and they asked if I could come to their house. When I walked in, the scene was no different than when I would respond to the death of a person. We sat and talked and prayed. I did what I could to comfort. Also, I offered my help with the burial. It's the family that's been left behind that needs our love and support.

What A Way To Go:

There was a woman in our Poplar Camp church who loved the Lord and was very faithful. Unfortunately, Ruby was diagnosed with cancer. I remember being at the Winston Salem hospital with all her large family for around eight hours on the day of her surgery. She later was admitted to the Wytheville Hospital and soon it became obvious that she was not going to make it. All of her family was in the waiting room and eventually in the hallway near her room. As she worsened they came into her room. Amazingly this lady remained totally conscious up to the minute of her passing. As she was nearing the end, she asked if everyone except her pastor and one family member would leave the room. I pulled up a chair beside her bed and held her hand. Suddenly she began to speak in a heavenly language until her last breath. You could feel the presence of the Lord in the room that day. Just think of what a miraculous thing it would be to leave this world speaking in a holy language that only God understands, only to wake up on the other side with Jesus.

Miracle in Sunday School Class:

We were in Sunday school at Poplar Camp when suddenly I heard some powerful rejoicing and praise coming from the adult class. In a few minutes they returned to the sanctuary and the Spirit spread all over the church. One of the women had come to church wearing a cast on her broken leg. She began to testify and declare that she had been healed. That night when she returned to church she was not wearing the cast. She had gone home and cut the cast off. She was walking fine and even today she shares this testimony. (I am not encouraging anyone to do this without God's unction.)

First One to Tell Me About Jesus:

A young man who I met many years ago, used to come to see his granddaddy who lived across the street from where we lived. Often, he would ring the doorbell and come in for a visit. He used to ask a lot of questions about the Bible but he simply did not understand the Scriptures. I talked with him and witnessed to him many times. He eventually went into the Marines and served our country. Years later, our paths crossed again in Lynchburg. I went to visit him and his wife and we began to talk about the Lord. It was then that he asked if I remembered talking with him about the Lord in those early days. I told him I certainly did. He told me that I was the first one to tell him about Jesus and the cross. Not many years later he went into the hospital and eventually passed away. I was called on to preach his funeral. Did I ever have a story to share!

Soul winning is one of the most rewarding things you can ever do. Just to feel like you had a tiny part in helping lead someone to Christ is most satisfying. Don't allow the enemy to convince you that your prayers are not effective and that your witnessing has been in vain. I implore you to continue sowing those seeds. One thing is for certain, if you don't sow the seeds you will not reap the harvest.

I Was There When It Happened:

There was a little lady at Lynchburg named Ann. Ann always worked hard at home and in the church. Something happened to her and she suddenly could not walk. It wasn't long before she had to go into a nursing home to take therapy. I visited with her and she was still not able to walk. One Sunday someone went to the nursing home, put her in a wheelchair and brought her into the service. I was shocked when I looked up and saw her. She said, "I've come for prayer for my healing." The church gathered around her and began to pray. All of a sudden, she jumped up from the wheelchair and began to walk around her chair. The power began to fall and when it hit her she took off running around the church crying out, "I'm healed! I'm healed!" It was one of the most awesome healings I can remember. They took her back to the nursing home and she walked in! The nurses were asking her what happened and she said, "God healed me." Some of the nurses were crying. I feel that same Spirit as I write. You don't have to be in church to be healed! Accept your healing by faith wherever you are.

10% Chance of Survival:

In October 2001, my wife was on stage singing with the praise team when suddenly she developed a severe headache. She said nothing about it to anyone, returned to her seat and waited until service ended. By then the pain was so severe that she asked me to take her home so she could lay down. We went home and she tried to lay down but she couldn't. She finally said, "I believe I need to go to the emergency room." As soon as she said that I knew we were in trouble. We arrived at the emergency room and they immediately began testing. Soon the young emergency room doctor told us that there was something serious going on and that he was calling in a specialist. They determined that she was bleeding on the brain. When the specialist arrived he immediately called the family together and said my wife had suffered an aneurism and would need immediate surgery. I asked him about her chances of survival and he said "10%." I asked what her chances of survival were if she did not have surgery. He said "0%." We agreed to proceed with the surgery. It was a difficult wait for sure but eventually the doctor came out and said the surgery had been completed but that she was going to suffer memory loss. When she began to wake up her memory was impaired. It was heart breaking but she was alive. She was eventually transferred to a room and in a few days was placed in a nursing home for therapy. Little by little she began to briefly remember things. Finally, it was time for her to come home. I was happy she was coming home but I was very apprehensive. How would I be able to keep an eye on her all day and night? The first night I put chairs across the hallway in case she tried to go to the lower level. She was confused and frustrated due to her memory loss. My son made some flash cards with things like, "What is your dog's name?" or "What are the names of your children?" She hated this little game but he did it over and over, trying to help her memory. Sometimes she would take two or three showers a day because she couldn't remember. Like most families, our family would come in at different times to eat. She thought she was supposed to eat each time one of us ate because she would forget she had already eaten.

I remember the first time she tried to fix breakfast. She had her cook book out to see how to fry an egg. She was very persistent and never gave up.

I had to be away one evening so I had a friend to come and stay with her while I was gone. I had turned off the breaker for the kitchen stove so she couldn't operate it due to her safety. When I returned I was surprised to see the stove was operating. She had led our friend to the breaker box and re-set the breaker. Also, while I was away she had taken several showers. When I walked in she did not look good. I asked her if something was wrong and she said, "I don't feel too good." I went upstairs and quickly saw why. Throughout the evening she had been going upstairs and eating candy…a whole box of Russel Stover candy!

She began to show signs of improvement so I took her to one of the Senior Saints meetings. She ate and it came time to play bingo. She had gone to get her a dessert and when she came back she sat in someone else's seat and started playing. She won. We all got a good laugh. And she was so happy to be a winner.

The "C" Word Strikes Home:

When my children were teenagers we used to have a lot of youth at our house. One night they all decided to go bowling and wanted me to go. I had never bowled so I finally decided to join them. When it came my turn, I got the ball down the lane and actually knocked over a few pins. By the time we finished the game my back started aching with pain. I immediately figured I had pulled a muscle from bowling. The pain was so great that I decided to go to the emergency room for an x-ray. The doctor said I indeed had strained a muscle. However, he said that he discovered a growth on my right kidney. I had no clue. After several scans they decided I would need surgery. The growth was cancerous. I had the surgery to remove a good portion of my right kidney and did well. That was in June, 2000. Looking back, had I not gone bowling that night and pulled a muscle requiring an x-ray, I wonder how long that growth would have grown…..perhaps too long. Romans 8:28 "And we know that all things work together for good to those who love God, to those who are the called according to *His* purpose." (NKJV)

The Dark Pit:

We were on our way to the General Assembly in Fort Worth Texas. I was excited because I had never been to Texas. We arrived safely and immediately joined with the massive crowd in worship. Every morning we met with our State Overseer for prayer. It was following one of those prayers that our State Overseer called my wife and I aside and said he needed to talk to us about being appointed as State Overseer of Virginia. My wife and I both broke out in tears. I asked for some time to pray about it and told him I would get back in touch with him. This was one of the most important decisions of my life. I had planned to spend that night alone with God while my wife went to the Assembly. As she was headed to the service she tripped and fell in the parking lot. I ran over to her to see if she was badly hurt. She was in a lot of pain and had to be taken to the emergency room. That was an all-night experience. Needless to say, I was unable to spend that time with God. Eventually I met with the Overseer again and after some pondering told him I would accept the position and was appointed.

I was so honored that the overseer had confidence and trust in me. I immediately began to feel torn between the new appointment and staying as pastor at the Lynchburg church. My emotions kept building and the battle kept raging inside. It finally came the day I was to go to State Headquarters to tour the facilities. I actually made myself go that day and never did feel at ease with being there. By now, the battle of the mind was raging. I started to have panic attacks and the tension had reached a peak level. I could not sleep and could not eat. Every morning I would wake up feeling stressed and the tension had reached a boiling point. I ended up in bed and battled day and night. I did not want to be around people and if I heard a car pull up in the driveway it caused terrific panic. I dreaded seeing night come and I dreaded seeing another day dawn. I reached a point where I felt worthless and without hope. The pressure was enormous. I spent days in that deep dark pit and there seemed to be no way out.

Finally, I decided that God wanted me to remain at Lynchburg as pastor. When the General Overseer called I told him I decided to continue pastoring and he relieved me of the appointment. I was out of my pulpit for a month or more. When I did return to church I started out sitting in the back with my wife. Eventually we kept moving up until finally I was on the front seat. It was at the end of one of the services that I finally walked into the pulpit and made some remarks. It wasn't long after that when I preached my first sermon.

That was in 1998 and I am still pastoring the Lynchburg church and I still have my precious wife by my side. He's a good, good Father.

Now That's Discipleship:

My daughter, Kristin, met a friend, Tracy, at high school and they were on the same basketball team. They became close friends and after a while Kristin invited her to church. She started coming regularly and fit right in. It wasn't long before she got saved. She went to youth camp and it was there she met one of our pastor's sons. They fell in love and are now serving in a church in North Carolina. While Tracy was still attending in Lynchburg, she mentioned that her sister would like to come and asked if I could pick her up. Sarah started attending, became a Christian and joined the church. After many years of bringing her with us on Sunday, a.m. and p.m. and Wednesday nights, she and her mother relocated to North Carolina. Sarah still stays in touch. This is how it is supposed to work. It's called personal evangelism. God shows up on time every time.

The Evening Concert:

I walked into mom's room at Medical Care Nursing Home one night and all the nurses on her wing were gathered around her. I thought her time had come to go to be with Jesus. I walked over and asked what was going on. They said, "Oh we come in here every evening and have Mrs. Vernon sing us some hymns." She was in the stage where she didn't even know our names most of the time. But guess what? She could sing every hymn and never miss a word. You tell me.

Healing In His Wings:

It was 2015 and we were at the State Convention. I was on program to preach the healing message entitled, "Healing in His Wings." There was a mighty anointing in the building that evening. At the end of the sermon we had a walk-through healing line. During this time one of my members came to me weeping. Obviously, she had seen something unusual, something miraculous.

As she was standing with her arm and hand outstretched toward the healing line, she was praying for people's healing. Suddenly, high above the beginning of the line, she saw what looked like a huge antique clay pitcher floating in the air. Suddenly it moved into a pouring position and floated over the heads of the people from the beginning of the line to the end, pouring out what appeared to be sparkling, shiny dust crystals!

Phyllis was amazed and was crying uncontrollably and sensed God's power was being poured out. This made such an impact on her that she tried to capture what she had seen in a sketch.

Church At The Furniture Store:

My middle brother ran a furniture store for many years. Don has always been easy going and easy to talk to. Every time I went to his store there was anywhere from two to five men who came by almost every day just to talk. My brother took every opportunity to talk to them about the Lord but they never showed much interest. He gave special attention to an elderly man named Frank. Frank and my brother become very good friends. Frank was way up in age but he was still making beautiful furniture. As time went on, Frank's health began to fail. Don kept talking to him about the Lord. Finally, he ended up in the hospital and my brother called and asked me to meet him there. Frank was in serious condition. When we arrived he was alert but very weak. I knew this would likely be our last chance to lead him to Christ. I talked to Frank and told him we had come to lead him to Christ. I asked him if he would be willing to pray the sinner's prayer. For the first time ever, he agreed. He repeated the prayer until we got about halfway through. He was going in and out of consciousness. I was on a mission. I told Frank we still had a little more and he agreed to finish the prayer. He accepted Christ right there in the hospital room. You could feel the presence of Almighty God as the burden lifted from him. Not only did the burden lift from him but also from my brother. He could finally rest in peace. Not long after his conversion, Frank went home to be with the Lord.

God deserves all the credit but I give my brother credit for being a kind, persistent, witness who softened his friend's heart in preparation for his final decision.

Six hours to live:

He was given six hours to live. Robert Hailey was on route to Fairfax, Virginia to deliver a truckload of stone. Back home in Lynchburg the truck dispatcher noticed by video that something was terribly wrong and radioed for Robert to pull over immediately. He managed to get stopped but was having a heart attack and fell getting out of the truck which resulted in a concussion. By the time help arrived Robert had to be resuscitated twice. He had not been breathing for 10-12 minutes.

During the days ahead he had surgery, receiving stents, broken ribs from the resuscitation, a COVID test (negative), A feeding tube, on a ventilator, body temperature brought very low, in a coma, blood clots, pneumonia, and was about to have tests on the brain. The doctor gave him about six hours to live.

After a previous attempt he finally began to wake up. He was just a little confused but he told his wife he loved her. Little by little he became more alert. The doctor that saw him the night he was brought into the emergency room, said it was amazing how far he had come.

Today he is at home and was back in church, along with his family. Yes, God does still perform miracles. I know because Robert, the miracle man, walked in Sunday. Amazing!

The Perfect Farewell:

I've seen some beautiful departures from this life over the years. My Deacon, Harvell Sullivan had one of the best planned goodbyes I ever witnessed. As he lingered through his last few days he remained alert. One by one each family member came by and he was permitted to talk to them alone and say goodbye. It wasn't planned but one would leave and another would come. This continued until he met with each one. Harvell and I had our final talk and he said he was going to be with the Lord. We discussed so many things and it was like the final chapter had been written and he said goodbye. I lost a very close friend and the church lost an outstanding deacon. Sometimes it seems that heaven picks the best but we will meet again.

THROUGH THE YEARS

Money Up In Smoke:

My dad was very strict while we were growing up. He even frowned on us reading the comics in the paper. (That didn't stop me from becoming a "Dennis the Menace.") Comic books were not to be left within view. I'm not sure how harmful Donald Duck and Porky Pig comics were but I know my oldest Brother Nyle had a nice stack of comic books which he kept hidden in his room. My brother had some first edition comic books and for some reason they disappeared. I always wondered if they ended up in the pot belly stove we had in the kitchen. Years later my brother started looking up the value of some of the first edition comic books he once had and found them to be worth thousands of dollars.

Put In My Three Cents:

I started tithing when I was a very young boy. I had swept out my Granddaddy's basement and he gave me a quarter. I asked my dad how much tithe I owed. He said, "two and one-half cents." He told me in a case like that he would just round it up. That's a principle I still use today. Back then, in quarterly conference they used to read out the tithes people had paid. Trust me, I would have been very disappointed if my three-cent tithe had not been recognized.

I have tithed all of my life but some years ago God prompted me to pay tithes on my **gross** income. I don't regret a cent I ever paid. God has been so good to me.

Child Bishop:

As a small boy, I loved to play cowboys, trucks and cars, play with my little farm set and ball. However, even as a small child I was interested in church. I played church a lot with my friends and it seemed that I was always selected to do the preaching. One thing led to another, and soon I appointed myself as "State Overseer." I carried my dad's old briefcase around the house and my favorite thing was appointing pastors. I remember appointing my dad to Cripple Creek. He got a kick out of that. I often wonder if he had any insight as to what was ahead.

Multipurpose Sink:

We did not get running water in the house for a few years. Even then, it was only a kitchen sink. We thought we had died and gone to heaven. Mom would wash her dishes and then put me in the sink and give me a bath. Uhhhh to the double use but I didn't particularly like the bath either.

We Had a Path:

We never did get an indoor bathroom when I was a young boy but we had one of the most modern outdoor Johnny houses in the country. It had duel seats and the seats had "store bought commode lids." How blessed can you be?

Hebrews 13:5 instructs us to be content with what we have. I can truthfully say that we were a contented family.

Big Mama:

One day my friend, Dennis and I decided to go to the little barn and see a new baby calf. We went in, stayed quite a while, petting and riding the calf. When we decided it was time to leave, we opened the door and there stood Old Jerz, mother of the calf, and she was not happy. She stood firmly at the door for a long time. Finally, when we could wait no longer, we jumped out the door past her. That was the fastest I ever ran in my life! Never underestimate the power of an **upset mother**.

Earn Your Living:

I was always trying to figure out a way to make a little money to spend at the grocery store up the hill from the house where we lived. I was touring the neighborhood looking for a fund raiser when I spotted a cherry tree full of cherries. I found a bucket, climbed the tree and filled the bucket with cherries. I still had to figure out a way to sell them. I spotted a house nearby, knocked on the door and asked the lady if she wanted to buy some cherries. She was very nice and gave me some change. It turns out she was a member of dad's church and the cherry tree belonged to her. Somehow word got back to my dad. I narrowly escaped a good ole country strappin'. He immediately called the member to apologize. She laughed and told him it was the cutest thing. I headed to the store whistling and anxious to spend my week's salary.

My First Funeral:

We were at the church most of the day for a funeral. In those days, they didn't have short funerals or short graveside services and they never got in a hurry. I paid special attention that day and when we got home my tricycle with a wagon built on the back became a hearse. Mr. "Locust Stick" had passed away and it was time to have his service. I found an old metal toy toolbox and that became the casket. I went through the whole process, preached the funeral, drove the body to the graveside, had the grave dug, shared a few words and then lowered the casket into the ground and filled up the grave, covering it with buttercups. Somewhere on the hill beside the Poplar Camp parsonage Mr. Stick's body still rests in peace to this day.

Unusual Requirement for Church Membership:

I became a member of the Poplar Camp Church of God of Prophecy on May 23, 1959. I clearly remember that service and how much I wanted to join. I kept moving up a seat at a time. Finally, I got the courage to ask my dad if I could join. Back then most people did not own a television. My neighbor purchased one and I was going over there watching cartoons and baseball games with her son. Dad knew that and was not happy. He took the opportunity to ask if I would stop going next door and watching television if I joined the church. I promised and joined. Sometime later I started wondering where in the Bible it said, "Thou shalt not watch TV?" Now over 60 years later I am wondering if he didn't have Divine insight.

God Knows Every Sparrow:

I was probably around 10 years of age before I was allowed to use a BB Gun. My friends were already going hunting with rifles and shotguns. My day finally came and I took off on my first hunting trip. Before long I spotted a little bird. I carefully aimed and shot, the little bird fell to the ground. I felt so guilty for what I had done that I cried and promised myself that I would never kill another bird. (Chickens not included.) I thought, that little bird could have a nest somewhere full of little baby birds waiting to be fed. To this day that is still painful for me to think about.

Bitter/Sweet:

When I was around 17 years old, I received a call from the military and they left the impression that I had to appear before the draft board on a certain date. Of course, I was a bit rattled and my mother was going nuts. I appeared on the date I was given and the recruiter made it sound like I was going to be drafted and tried to get me to sign up early. I was upset and nervous about the whole situation. I called the draft board to find out more information. A very nice lady asked me to come and talk with her. She wanted to know what they told me. It turns out that it was a recruiter trying to sign up young men for the army. The lady told me that she would be speaking to him about the situation and she was upset with how he handled things. She asked me what I was doing. I told her I was working eight hours a night, going to school and pastoring a church on the weekend. She said, "you are pastoring a church now?" I said "yes." She said, "I am going to classify you as 4D and you should not hear from us again or from the draft board." Did I just happen to be at Winfall church or was I there for a purpose? I never did hear from them again and I still have that deferral card just in case they change their minds.

I'm in the Army now:

Over the years, I have always admired the people who serve in the military. I have very deep respect for them and always tell them so. Since my encounter with that recruiter, there has always been an emptiness in my heart. It's like I missed something that I should have done. To this day that emptiness remains. Once this was really bothering me and I began to pray about it and asked God to help me win victory over these feelings. During that prayer God sent these words: "Why are you fretting over this? You have been serving in the greatest army on earth since you were seven. You have steadily moved up in the ranks and one day you will be a captain in this army." I had never looked at it that way and it certainly encouraged me. However, when I see a soldier in uniform I still wonder if I missed a little part of my life.

The Immaculate Room:

Before going to one church in the state my dad told me that the pastor and his wife were very nice people but very particular. He told me to keep my room clean and tidy. I don't know how my dad knew that information but he was right. The first day I was told what time breakfast was to be served and it was very early. I told the pastor's wife that was fine and I would be at breakfast. After I ate breakfast I told them I was going to my room for a time of meditation and prayer with God. (I learned this from the many evangelists who stayed in our home.) Soon as that door was closed, I laid back down and finished my eight hours of sleep. When I got out of bed the second time I cleaned every inch of the room, hung up my clothes neatly, and made up my bed until it was perfect all the way around. (I'm glad my mom didn't know I could do those things.) The pastor's wife would come in behind me, check every corner and make sure there was not a wrinkle. I thought, "You may do all of that but you will not find a wrinkle." These two people were so wonderful to me. When my dad saw them for the first time after the revival the pastor told him that I was the neatest evangelist they ever had. I'm pretty sure my dad found that hard to believe based on what it was like when I came home between revivals.

Working for a Millionaire:

When I was a boy in Lynchburg we had some neighbors, who were millionaires. They drove a nice big Cadillac and lived in a huge house with a two-car garage.

One day the wife called me and wanted to know if I would come and pick cherries off their cherry tree. I told her I would. At the time I had no income and I was going to work for a millionaire! I climbed the tree and picked a bucket of cherries. It took a little longer than I anticipated. Of course, I was eating about every other cherry. It was time for me to deliver the goods. The lady was very nice and thanked me over and over, but she didn't give me any money. I left so disappointed. My dream of getting rich was gone. Later that evening she came to our house and when I saw her coming my hopes were restored. Instead, she had brought us one of the best cherry cobblers I have ever tasted. It was delicious! It didn't replace that dollar or two I was hoping to get but it was good. **Now**, at my age, I would *pay her* to have one of her cobblers. My, how our taste changes with time.

A son, Jason Edward Vernon, was born in Danville on November 16, 1976. He weighed just 4lb and 8oz and I could hold him in my hand.

He was married to Casey Prince and they have two sons, Isaac and Holden. They live in Gainsville, Ga. where he works for Jentzen Franklin at Free Chapel. He has brought great joy to us.

A Daughter is Born: During our pastorate at Poplar Camp, God blessed us with a second child, Kristin Leigh Vernon, born in Radford July 8, 1981.

She brought much joy into our home.

She married Jim Whitford and they have two sons, Addison and Carson.

My Kidnapped Daughter:

This story brings back some bitter memories. We were in Roanoke and decided to go to the Towers Mall. It was Alma, Jason, Kristin, my mom and me. Jason had gotten interested in collecting baseball cards so we decided to go to the card shop and look around. The rest of the group went to shop. As Jason and I were looking at the cards, I suddenly missed Kristin. I asked Jason where his sister was and he said he had not seen her. My wife had told me that Kristin was going with them but I did not hear her say that. I went into a massive panic mode and told Jason we were going to look for her. We literally ran through every store, both levels until I could not run any longer. I was out of breath and could not go another step. I must have looked terrible because a woman stopped and asked me if I was ok. At that moment, I looked up and saw my mom, my wife and Kristin headed toward us. They were happy and talking as usual, not knowing the anxious moments we had endured. I was so thankful to God to see my daughter safe.

Good communications are essential. In everything we do we need to establish good communications to avoid conflict. Having a good understanding is always a must.

Welcome New Pastor: The first Sunday we were at Danville I walked through the front door and there was an older gruff-looking man in the entrance foyer. I reached out to shake his hand and the first thing he said was, "you won't make it here for one month!" (And "welcome to you too" brother.) The next person I met was his wife. I reached out to shake her hands and she pulled back her hand and said, "I don't shake hands." (I later learned that she had a problem with her hand.) As time went on this elderly couple became wonderful friends. They gave us all the food we could pick out of their garden and we even took a trip or two with them.

An Amazing Lady:

I want to introduce you to an amazing lady named Rhea Austin. Rhea was one of the most intelligent and talented women I ever met. She was on her way to becoming a school teacher until in her youth she developed crippling arthritis. She lived with her mother and soon became bed ridden. In spite of her hands being turned inward, she never complained about her constant pain. However, in her condition, she became a beautiful artist; painting with the brush stuck between her fingers. She also learned to play the keyboard with her twisted hands. She taught Sunday school and was a very good Bible scholar. Her talents were amazing!

She wanted to be baptized and we had to figure out how we could do that. We finally decided to sit her in a chair and baptize her and the chair together. The day of her baptism it was cold outside and there were traces of ice along the creek banks. She wanted to be dipped three times.

She did fine and never was affected by the cold water.

Finders, Keepers:

My two older brothers were at the age when their interest was in cars and girls. Long ago they had laid their toys aside and now I was the beneficiary. Not only was I blessed to have all their clothes passed down to me, but I had all the toys. I want to tell you about two of them. I was looking through some boxes one day and I happened to see an old box that a telephone had come in. When I opened it, I found a box of baseball cards. I took those cards out and played with them quite a bit. In fact, one of my brothers showed me how to take a clothes pin and attach it to my bike so, as the spokes on the wheel turned, it sounded like a motorcycle. I wonder now, which cards and how many cards I destroyed. Anyhow, I kept them over the years and when my son was born we started collecting. We had some great father/son times together. I was looking through those cards some time back and found Mickey Mantle, Roger Marris, Yogi Berra, and many others. If I had taken good care of them they would have been worth a lot of money. When I brought this up with my brothers, they tried to reclaim them for their own.

I really hit the jack pot when I found a box of marbles from the early fifties. When they looked at them they started picking out the marbles they remembered. I wonder how important those girls and cars are now! Sorry, your loss, my gain. If I had to wear your hand-me-down clothes I also get your hand-me-down toys.

At 4 years of age, little did I know that three years later I would preach my first sermon.

FUNNY THINGS HAPPEN IN THE MINISTRY

The Open House:

We lived in a country house with no indoor plumbing and no furnace. That house got so cold upstairs where us boys slept that you could see your breath. One night my oldest brother, Nyle, was drinking a Pepsi and had about half a bottle left. The next morning, it was frozen. We had a little wood stove in the kitchen and an oil heater in the living room. My mom would cover us with so many quilts that you had to get in the position you wanted to sleep because once she finished there was no turning. We carried water from the spring and all of us drank water from the same bucket and with the same dipper. Seldom were we sick and we were happy. When I think about that old parsonage, I cannot help but thinking about the Scripture in Matthew 22:14 where Jesus tells us that "**many are called**, but **few are chosen**." My interpretation to that Scripture is, *"Many are cold, but few are frozen."*

I'm Superman:

I'm already chuckling as I share a story about my brother Don. Don was always adventurous and you had to watch what you dared him to do. I remember him going into the house and getting mom's umbrella. I believe he was playing Superman and climbed on top of the shed and jumped off with the umbrella that was supposed to help him fly. He was faster than a speeding bullet. You guessed it. The umbrella went straight up and he went straight down…hard! But we were having fun!

Your Sins Will Find You Out:

Our next-door neighbor had a milk cow and often when they were overstocked with milk, she would bring us milk in a jar. My dad loved it but us boys had gotten used to drinking homogenized milk and refused to drink the fresh milk. One night my oldest brother got thirsty and went downstairs to get something to drink. When he entered the kitchen, much to his surprise, daddy was pouring the fresh milk out of the jar into the homogenized milk carton. No telling how long we had been drinking what we called, "real milk." Dad was caught!

The Smoking Seat:

My second-grade teacher was Mrs. Umberger. I never was a mean person but I was very mischievous. We had taken a bathroom break and my friend, Mike and I kept lingering in there. She would holler in the door and tell us to come out. Every time she would call us we would say, "you can't come in yet!" Finally, she had all she could take and she said, "I'm coming in to get you." She came in, took us to the classroom, brought us up in front of the whole class, had us bend over at the blackboard, and paddled us with a paddle. It was one of the hardest whippings I can ever remember. Trust me, we never pulled that trick again.

"Near-Drowning" at Baptismal:

My dad baptized me in a creek. He always went out first with a stick to test the water, poking the stick looking for deep places. This time he tapped the stick and many little baby snakes came swimming to the top of the water. It was one of the most spirited baptismal services ever! When it came my turn to be baptized, so help me, I thought my dad held me under for two to three minutes. I guess he was hoping it would cleanse me of my mischievousness. Actually, about the only change was that I went down a dry mischievous boy and came up a wet mischievous boy.

"Spirits" at the Parsonage:

We had chickens, guineas, a dog, a possum, a duck and hogs while dad pastored Poplar Camp church. When one of dad's members said, "I brought you a chicken," it was not cut up or wrapped in cellophane. It was in a box pecking at the top and trying to escape. I loved the animals and liked feeding them. One day one of my brothers picked up a whisky bottle someone had thrown away, that still had some whisky left in it. I never asked what his original intent was. Anyhow, he poured it in a bowl and set it down on the ground. Before long, a big rooster came and drank some of that white lightening. He started staggering and swaying and trying to crow. Of course, we got a good laugh from it. I'm not sure if that was the next chicken my dad killed for supper. Animal lovers, please don't send me complaints. I love animals, but you know "kids will be kids!"

When Life is not Fair:

Growing up, my brother, Don, finally had a car and was driving. He came in one day and, untypical of him, started talking back to my dad. It rubbed my dad wrong and he pulled off that size 48 belt and reared back to thrash him. My brother told him he was not going to whip him anymore and he jerked the belt out of his hand. My dad fell on his knees and wept. A few years later I had moved up in the world and was driving an old '52 Plymouth. One day my dad and I were standing in the same place where my brother and dad had stood, and the same thing happened. I remembered the incident with my brother and I said, "Dad, you are not going to whip me again." Only thing, instead of him dropping to the floor to pray it was me who was getting up off the floor. I went to my room and cried for a while. I was feeling sorry for myself and wondering what I did differently than my brother. Life is just sometimes not fair.

An Itchy Sermon:

My Granddaddy, W.M. Lowman, was scheduled to speak at the Poplar Camp church on a Sunday. His sermon was entitled "The Vine and the Branches." He asked me to go into the woods and cut him a grapevine to use for an illustration in his sermon. I was so excited that I got to do something for my granddaddy! Off to the woods I went with a hatchet and right off I saw a long vine hanging from a tree. I immediately cut a piece about one foot long and hurried home with it. He thanked me. The next morning, I woke up itching my hands, arms, and face. That was not a grapevine I had cut but it was poison oak. I think my Granddaddy was *itching* to get into the pulpit that day.

Defending My Testimony:

When I was in middle school in Lynchburg there were some bullies always on the prowl. I tried to stay away from them but they would find me. School was about to begin one morning and we were standing outside. One of the boys started accusing me of using bad language, while hollering it out to the assembled crowd. I told him I didn't but he kept on. I couldn't let him destroy my testimony. I had to defend myself. Before I knew it, we were in a fist fight. It finally ended and that boy never bothered me again. At the time, I felt vindicated. I had stood my ground defending my testimony. The problem was that while I was defending my testimony, I lost it.

My Dad Saved My Life:

We returned from our honeymoon trip and arrived at our apartment in Brookneal. It was past time for us to eat dinner so Alma went into the kitchen and I stretched out on our used sofa. We had a small black & white TV with an indoor antenna so I flipped it on and starting watching a program. I remember thinking, married life is so cool. About that time, I heard my wife sniffing in the kitchen. I couldn't imagine what was wrong. Was it possible she was homesick? I got up to see what was happening and when I stepped into the kitchen she was crying. I asked what was wrong. She said, "I CAN'T COOK." I told her not to worry. I knew how to fix a hamburger and boil wieners to make hotdogs. I could even fix a bowl of cereal. She finally settled down and everything was fine until time for the next meal. What does all of this have to do with dad saving my life? My dad must have experienced a Divine revelation because he gave us a brand-new Betty Crocker cook book. It wasn't long before she was cooking and boy, what a good cook she was! I gained far too much weight. That problem had been solved, or had it?

When my wife had her aneurism she lost all her memory and guess what that included? Cooking. Well I became the chief cook for a while but eventually she picked up where she left off. If at first you don't succeed then try again.

Returns on Giving:

While we were living in Lynchburg, I felt impressed to send my dad $100. You may think that wasn't much money but, in those days, it was. Alma and I had worked hard for that money. When we got home I went to the mailbox and got my bank statement. It showed that I had $100 deposited into my account. To this day I do not have a clue how that got into my account. I went to the bank and all they could tell me was the day it was deposited. I wrote my dad and told him how God had replaced the money I gave to him. In a few days I received a letter from him that said, "Dear Son, why don't you try it again!"

Tough Decision:

When we brought Jason home he didn't even weigh five pounds. We had a poodle who was very jealous and walked around whining because he was not getting attention. Jason was crying constantly day and night and Alma and I had reached our limit. One morning I jokingly said, "We have to get rid of the dog or the baby." Alma said, "Let me think about it." We both laughed. We eventually found the dog a good home. (Sorry Jason, I've never shared this story with you.

Wait! Wait:

While pastoring in Danville I was asked to perform a wedding for an 87 year old man and an 86 year old woman. They both attended my church. On the day of the wedding the old man walked into the church and was very excited. He was well dressed but he had cut himself shaving with a razor. I took him to the dining area and started scrubbing his shirt. It dried just in time for the wedding to begin. The wedding went smoothly and afterwards we went to the dining room for the reception.

All of the people had gathered and were watching. The photographer was about to take a picture of the bride and groom but the man hollered out and said, "wait! wait!" Then he proceeded to reach into his pocket, took out his false teeth, put them in, smiled and said "ok, go ahead."

What Did You Say?:

While pastoring in Danville I continually had trouble keeping a teacher for the Women's Class. The problem was not the teacher but an elderly student who liked to talk constantly while the teacher was teaching. Finally, I asked my mother to teach that class and she agreed. On the way home after teaching her first lesson I asked her how things went. She said, "I didn't have any trouble at all. When I got up to teach I turned off my hearing aid." Something tells me the class had two teachers that day.

We are Blessed in Different Ways:

We had gathered for church and had been blessed in the service. Our next-door neighbor, Wiley, had come in late and you could smell alcohol. He stayed until the end of the service and I was talking about how the Lord had blessed us. Wiley had been sitting there and was just clapping his hands over and over. I said, "Even Wiley back there was getting a blessing." Wiley spoke up loudly and said, "getting a blessing nothing…them blame gnats are about to worry me to death." So, ended the service.

Batman:

One night we were in service and I was beginning to really get anointed by God until people spotted a bat flying around the sanctuary. I quickly lost their attention. They were watching the bat and I was getting very frustrated. I decided I would go on with the sermon so I told everyone to ignore that bat and tune back in. I had no more said that when the bat flew directly toward me at the podium. I quickly ducked down behind the Bible stand said, **"Somebody get that bat out of here!"** Some of the men coaxed it into the basement and took care of it. In the mean time I tried to finish my sermon but suddenly realized it had already ended when that bat flew in.

Just leave it Alone:

Once I was preaching a sermon on "Seeking for that which is lost until you find it." I used something that happened a few days earlier as an example. I lost my calendar with a year of important dates inside. I looked the house over, turned the sofa upside down, checked in all the chairs and had basically combed the entire house. Then I said, "I walked by the *SECRETARY* and rubbed my hand across it and *SNAP*; just like that I remembered where I had left it." People started laughing more and more when I said, "I remembered when I ran my hand across the secretary." When I realized what they were laughing at I was so embarrassed and tried to clear it up by saying, "No, no, you have the wrong idea. I'm talking about the kind of secretary with drawers." It was over at that point! Sometimes better to leave things alone than to try to correct them when you are embarrassed.

My Birthday Suit:

The church gave me a new suit for my birthday, so the following Sunday I wore it. Our song director got up and was talking about my birthday. Everything was fine until she looked around at me before the whole congregation and said, "I think my pastor looks really good in his birthday suit." The laughter started and I dared not try to explain it. My face was already red with embarrassment.

A New Form of Worship?

Another time I was preaching my heart out to those in the congregation. About ten minutes into the sermon I began to notice that everyone in unison would lift up their heads and then in unison they would put their heads down. This went on for some time, it was really distracting me but I pressed on. After service I asked what was going on and someone said, "a spider was building a web from the altar up to the curtain rod and back." Their heads were following him up and back down. They said that every few minutes I would go right in front of the web and as I preached would point my finger right through the middle of it. The distractions that can happen during a sermon……..

My Golf Career:

My golfing career was brief but very remarkable. My good friend, Tommy, who was the funeral director of the local funeral home, invited me to go play golf one day. I decided I would go but I warned him that I had never played golf before. We got there and right off, I had no clubs. I also didn't know one club from another. Tommy spent some time explaining the game but suddenly we had another problem. I couldn't hit the ball. After awhile, I was able to hit the ball but it never went where I needed it to go. Tommy was very patient with me but the people behind us didn't seem too happy for some reason. Anyhow, we finally made it through and headed home. I don't recall how high my score was but it was quite high. Of course, Tommy's score was quite low. We pulled up at the house and my wife came out and asked how I did. I told her the score and she got all excited and asked, "How in the world did you beat Tommy?" My conscience wouldn't allow me to hide the truth and I had to tell her the low score was the winner. For some strange reason Tommy never asked me to play golf again!

Our Unwelcome Visitor:

My wife, Jason and I were sitting in the den in the Poplar Camp parsonage quietly watching TV with the den glass sliding door open and the screen door closed so we could enjoy the night fresh air. All of a sudden, I looked at the door through the screen and saw a skunk standing there just looking at us. It was like he was listening to the TV. I whispered, "Be really quiet and don't anybody move." It was then that Jason **Loudly** said, "***WHY DADDY, WHATS WRONG?***" We were deeply blessed that night that we were not sprayed with skunk perfume. Why is it that when you tell people not to do something it triggers them to do it? Thank God for the sweet-smelling Savior.

The Fig Leaf Story:

One Sunday I had just gotten up to preach and I noticed that several people began to snicker. I sensed something was wrong. You got it, my zipper was down. There I was, knowing they had already seen the malfunction, so while continuing to preach I was trying to decide what to do. I finally decided the only place around to fix my problem was behind the Bible stand so I went over and thought I had tactfully corrected the malfunction. About that time, I heard more snickering and now *really* wondered what was going on. Well, it so happened that at that time we had our nursery behind the platform. We had put a two-way mirror glass in the big window so people could not see in but those in the nursery could see out. That window was like a big mirror behind me and the congregation had a bird's eye view, not to mention that the nursery workers could see out. I guess it happens to the best of them.

Did you know God works at a fast food place?

My wife and I had been visiting all day and it was way past lunch time. We pulled into Burger King and were sitting there talking about what we would order. I just happened to check my front pocket where I keep my cash and realized that I did not have one cent with me. (Not even a credit card.) I told my wife I was sorry but we would just have to wait. About that time Donald and Ava, a couple I had pastored at Winfall many years before, pulled right up beside my car and we talked for a few minutes. Donald got out of his car and walked right over to me and handed me money, got back in his car and left. They had no clue of our predicament. My wife and I went inside and ordered two Whopper value meals, and they sure tasted good! Yes, God even works at fast food restaurants!

Memorized Testimony:

There is an elderly gentleman who has been coming to the Lynchburg church since he was a small boy. Doyle has been very faithful over the years. For many years he always asked to testify at some point in the service. His testimony was always word for word the same. Everyone in the church could quote his testimony. This one particular service he started testifying, got through about the second line and totally went blank. I was standing in the pulpit and without even thinking spoke the next line of his testimony word for word. He said, "yes that's it," and finished his testimony. It was a light moment I'll always remember.

From The Mouth Of Babes:

When my daughter Kristin started school in Lynchburg she was excited about her first class. The teacher decided to find out something about the students and their parents, so she asked Kristin what kind of work her daddy did and she answered, "He doesn't work, he's a preacher!" Needless to say, that first PTA meeting was interesting.

Don't Try This at Home:

I have never drank a beer or tasted alcoholic beverages. I have never smoked a cigarette or used tobacco. However, I do want to make a confession. This experience happened at Granddaddy and Grandmother's house on Front Street in Salem, Virginia. My brother and his first cousin had set up a little make-shift tent in the back yard. My curiosity got the best of me and I went inside the tent and found a bunch of hollow sticks about the size of a cigarette and it did not take me long to figure out what was going on. Soon I found matches. I decided, "I think I will try one." I put the stick in my mouth, lit it and took one big puff. In the process, I sucked fire down my throat and it burned for a long time. I never touched anything that looked like a cigarette again. I often wondered if that incident convinced me to never smoke. Ok, you have the scoop on me. Now go have fun with it. Attention! Do not try this at home!

My First Photography Course:

My Uncle Dudley was a wonderful man that I looked up to very much but he was VERY particular. One evening, he was going into the darkroom to develop film and print pictures and I begged him to let me watch. He reluctantly agreed and he explained that we would be in there for some time and couldn't turn on the light. I was so excited and couldn't wait for him to get started. About half way through I needed to go the bathroom but he was so particular and I was afraid I would ruin his pictures. I believe we stayed in there a little longer than he said and eventually I wet my pants…..enough for a puddle to form on the floor. (The rain came down and the floods came up.) When he finally finished and turned on the light he immediately saw the puddle and asked what happened. I told him I didn't want to ruin his pictures. He didn't ever mention it again and I eventually learned from him how to develop film, print pictures and I later even had my own darkroom. I have loved photography since.

Where is My Pet Duck:

When I was a small boy I found a baby duck in the field and decided to bring it home and try to save it. After a little arguing with mom, she agreed for me to keep it. I fed it every day and it began to grow. Then I started digging up fishing worms and feeding Quacky. The duck grew very big and beautiful and was a wonderful pet. It followed me wherever I went. I came in one day from school and my duck was gone. I still am not sure what happened to that duck but later I heard that one of my dad's members had duck for Thanksgiving. I would later pastor that member. I decided to let ducks be by-ducks.

Children are a Heritage of the Lord:

Bishop Allen Davis was serving as State Overseer of Virginia and was coming to the Poplar Camp church for his first visit since I had become pastor. Naturally, you want everything to go just right. The service went well and we had a nice crowd. I was starting to feel a little relief from the pressure. Church had ended and we walked into the parsonage. When we stepped inside I asked everyone to be seated in the living room. Everyone did except my son, Jason. When he disappeared I had an uneasy feeling. In about three to four minutes he came running into the living room and first asked why we were sitting in there rather than the den. I said, "son, we are just going to sit here and talk for a little while." He then said, "The Jefferson's are on." I said I don't care about that. Then he said, "I thought you said it was your favorite show?" By then I was embarrassed. The State Overseer got me off the hook when he stood and said, "come on Jason, I'll go watch the Jefferson's with you." We all went to the den and watched….you guessed it….The Jeffersons.

RECOGNITION OF THREE SPECIAL MENTORS

Raymond Carpenter was a member of the Poplar Camp church when I was a young boy and was still there when I went back years later to pastor. He was such a loving and wise man and knew the Scripture thoroughly. He was a counselor to me and a great encourager, and always found something good to say about every sermon I preached. One Sunday, my sermon was a disaster and I knew it. So did he. So, what did he say about *that* sermon? He shook my hand and said, "Brother Gary, you picked out a great Scripture for your sermon today." Never will I forget my final visit with him in the hospital. He was declining rather rapidly and part of his family was in the room as we began to pray. The Holy Ghost filled that room. There was a message and interpretation given that said, "It is well, my child, it is well with your soul." It was heart rending and we all wept. When things settled he looked up and said, "so this is the way it's going to be, is it?" It wasn't long before he went to be with Jesus. I had the honor of preaching his funeral.

Buena Mitchell was a member of the Winfall church. I was so moved when she told me about her place of prayer behind the house where they lived. Every time she went to pray she would carry a rock with her and put it on the rock pile before she prayed. I saw this pile of rocks and it touched my heart to know that each rock represented a prayer request. I still miss chatting with her even today, but she moved to higher ground. I was honored to preach her funeral.

Vernil Sides, who was a faithful pastor for many years in Alabama, had me conduct a revival when I was in my teens. It was during that week that God gave me two new lifetime friends. Brother and Sister Sides had lost their first baby named "Gary." Sister Sides said, "They were just going to adopt me into the family" and that's exactly what happened.

Brother Sides was a great soul winner and a strong witness for Christ. We grew closer and closer over the years. The last four years of his life were spent in Lynchburg, Virginia with his daughter Phyllis and his son-in-law, Sherwood. This man would preach to anybody who would listen. He had such a sweet spirit that people were drawn to him. He was one of the greatest personal soul winners I ever met. Like Brother Carpenter, he was a great encourager. I was so sad to lose my friend but He had a great home-going. I was privileged to speak at his funeral in Alabama. I called him "Our modern-day Apostle Paul."

THE LOVE OF MY LIFE

This book is dedicated to my childhood sweetheart and my lovely wife, Alma. At the time of this writing we are nearing our 50th anniversary. Alma is a wonderful companion, a great pastor's wife, an outstanding mother and Nana and most of all a solid, faithful Christian example. She has always stood by my side throughout our life together. Our years together have been peaceful, loving, and beautiful. Our marriage has been built on trust and commitment. Alma is an amazing lady who loves the Lord. She reads the Bible through every year without fail. All the people from the churches I have pastored have always loved Alma and have shown her a lot of respect.

She gets up singing Christian choruses every day. Ninety eight percent of the time wherever you see me, you see Alma. I'm so glad God brought us together. It is just another way *He interwove our lives together as one.* God had my wife picked out for me long before I knew her. Thank you, God, for such a beautiful gift!

God has blessed me with an amazing life and a wonderful ministry.

I consider it to be the most honorable thing on earth to be called by God to be a shepherd. I have pastored some of the greatest people on earth and each of my ministries, from my first sermon at seven to the six churches where I pastored over the past 50 years have been rewarding.

I've had a tonsillectomy, removal of one-half of my thyroid, gall bladder removal, heart attack, stent in heart, complete nervous breakdown, numerous kidney stones, rotor cuff surgery, diabetes, sleep apnea, stroke, COVID 19, and removal of part of my kidney due to cancer. I'm breathing and alive and grateful that God has kept me.

"Twas grace that brought me safe thus far, and grace will lead me on"

He has a plan for my life and He will continue putting the pieces together until it is complete.

One of the most rewarding things as a pastor is when you feel you have helped save a marriage, played a role in helping a young person get off drugs, led a soul to Christ, baptized new converts, offered comfort during times of loss and mentored those who seek guidance.

That has been my life.

Conclusion:

Something different, something new, something we have never experienced before is taking place right before our eyes. Our country is shifting gears, attitudes are changing, respect is lacking for one another, but we must not be dismayed or allow the enemy to deceive us in our final journey home. People get ready, for Jesus has promised to return for His Church. Look around you. Surely you can clearly see the signs pointing to His coming.

The bottom line, the line that matters most, is not where you go to church, how long you have been a member, what leadership positions you held or how many times you have been baptized. No, the bottom line is, "Is it well with your soul?"

If your heart is not prepared to meet God, bow your head right now and say, "Jesus, I'm not the worst person on earth but I have sinned against God. I'm sorry for the sins I have committed and I invite you to come into my heart, forgive me of my sins and set me free in Jesus name. Lord I promise to change my habits that are not pleasing to you and beginning today, I will serve you faithfully as long as I live."

God has a plan for you. Allow him to start *weaving the strands of your life* until you have finished your course and fulfilled His will.

ABOUT THE AUTHOR

He was born into a family with ten ministers and was raised in a pastor's home. From early childhood he knew he was destined to become the next minister. He always had a passion for God and for ministering to the weak, the sick, the hurting and especially the lost. He is known for having the heart of a shepherd.

Printed in the United States
by Baker & Taylor Publisher Services